Lost Ireland

Laurence O'Connor

lost Ireland

A photographic record at the turn of the century with an introduction and commentary by Patrick Gallagher

RAINBOW

CRESCENT BOOKS
New York

First published 1984 by Rainbow Publications Ltd.

Copyright © Rainbow Publications Ltd., 1984.

This 1984 edition is published in the U.S.A. by Crescent Books, distributed by Crown Publishers, Inc.

ISBN 0 - 517 - 453940

ACKNOWLEDGEMENTS

'Dublin' reprinted by permission of Faber and Faber Ltd. 1966 from The Collected Poems of Louis MacNeice

'Ireland with Emily' by John Betjeman reprinted by permission of John Murray (Publishers) Ltd. 1962

Originated and produced by Rainbow Publications Ltd.
Design by Liam Miller
Photoset in Plantin type and assembled by
Design & Art Facilities (Photosetting) Limited, Dublin
Printed in Great Britain by Robert Hartnoll Ltd.

Foreword

The following pages of images from the past in Ireland are a segment of a collection which has taken me upwards of thirty years to accumulate. In this selection I have endeavoured to show changes in the quality of life in day-to-day living in Ireland spanning almost a century through the eye of the camera.

The fifties were a marvellous valley period between the immediate aftermath of the War and the economic lift-off of the sixties. Dublin, with its secondhand bookshops, its house auctions and junk shops, was a vast Aladdin's Cave of everything old.

If you were not too concerned with the problems of day-to-day living in the fifties, one could, as I did, get into the past of this country and this capital city of ours.

The topographical gems one could pick up in the then more abundant bookshops in the city, the sheer joy of finding an old photograph or photographic plate with maybe the image of a face frozen in time looking at you from a familiar street corner, or yet another showing an old streetscape long gone to rubble. This interest, for me, took much of the hardship out of the fifties.

To me, life looks pleasant in many of these photographs. There were drawbacks – the grim poverty of many of the people, the bad roads – but the general impression is of uncrowded trams, side-cars, people moving easily through the traffic and in some instances stopping to talk in the middle of the road. The whole flavour arouses a certain envy today.

If these pictures stimulate the reader's nostalgia, as they did mine, I feel my efforts will have been more than rewarded.

Laurence O'Connor

Patrick Gallagher 1842–1922
b. Enniscorthy, County Wexford; d. Macroom, Co. Cork

Introduction

One of my grandfathers, whose name is also mine, was born in the year 1842. He was thrice-married, by inclination a rose-grower and fisherman, by occupation the sergeant of police in the sleepy town of Macroom in the south of Ireland. Quite recently my father, who was also born in the nineteenth century, rediscovered a tiny chipped sepia snapshot of the old man, about one-and-a-half inches square. When professionally enlarged, that scrap of sensitized paper became my introduction to my ancestor.

Although that photograph does not of course come from the Laurence O'Connor collection, I have asked the publisher to place it modestly on this page, for reasons germane to this introduction and close to what I suspect is the cast of Mr O'Connor's mind. For there is an element of, yes, 'devilry' in photography, something magical about the way an old album can display and expose the walking dead. Old photographs are spooks left by their subjects, emanations of their presence, tracings of their bodies. They are not at all one man's image of another, as is the painted portrait. They are tangible after-images of existence: they diminish imagination, offering in its place an embarrassing closeness to the waxy dead.

I have not had the pleasure of meeting Mr Laurence O'Connor but feel that he of all people will understand my idiosyncratic compulsion to have that old Munster sergeant gaze out at us. It is that continuing business of magic. We only destroy images when they become too powerful for their own good, or for our good. Normally we treat them with decent respect, shivering to break a mirror, reluctant to tear up a photograph. Within a day of the O'Connor archive coming into my knowledge, my grandfather's stern image swam up through a developer's tank and slowly fixed itself on some special paper. I do not much care how it was done; the coincidence was there, diablerie was in the air.

As he hints but does not say in his foreword, Mr O'Connor was aware when making his collection that his was a sacredotal function. To collect with no view to reward is a felicity given to few. Dublin has always been lucky in its antiquaries, its appointed magpies. The curious may conjure up the O'Connor household: books, prints, plates, maps, scrolls, deeds, magazines, newspapers, almanacks, brochures, catalogues, tickets, programmes, records, cylinders, stereoscopes and James Joyce's bicycle clips.

This salvager extraordinary describes the joy of collection in the fifties of this century when in Ireland there was a considerable diaspora of goods and chattels. The contents of camera-houses in forgotten estates were finding their way to the market. Was Mr O'Connor lucky enough to have attended the great sales at Cahir or Carton, or the auction at Doneraile Court, days of mythic buying? No matter; this book shows he was in many a right place at many a right time, and we are lucky his nameless cast of country and city people, rankers and filers mostly, survived to form this orderly community of rescued ghosts.

Not that there was anything at all tidy, much less correct, about the society these photographs reflect. From the famines of the 1840s to independence of a sort around 1920, the population of Ireland halved. A great deal of what Victorian travellers chose to see as Hibernian whimsy or Celtic mist was in fact the miasma of a reeking poverty. That poverty, so specific in so many of these photographs, was part of the stock-in-trade of an Irish continuum that was damaging and unnatural. England was immensely powerful, Ireland intolerably poor; the whole thrust of Westminster policy was to suppress Irish disaffection and to shy away from any accommodation with the Irish problem lest the timbers of a still seaworthy Empire should begin to shiver. It was not that England disliked her western neighbour but rather that behind the Irish she dimly discerned peoples of a darker hue and losses of an inconceivable magnitude.

There were always hundreds of articulate Irish who would not put up with the wretchedness, and did not hesitate to scourge the causes of it; but there were also tens of thousands of inarticulate Irish who had no choice but to put up with it. Juxtapose a stinking Dublin tenement courtyard, probably owned *sub rosa* by an elected Catholic city councillor, and a sagging bog cottage on the estate of an absentee aristocrat, and you see the two sides of the Queen's shilling, that dud Victorian coin that rang falsely all through the period covered by this collection. This whole collection is political, yet the only deliberately propagandist images here are the series highlighting city poverty.

It is almost certain that the Irish literary renaissance could not have occurred had the electricity of political agitation not generated the necessary energy. The photographs in these pages have no direct relevance to literature, but Joyce's Dublin is there in plain view and the sequences

8

from the Aran Islands are not at all unlike the pictures Synge himself took there between 1898 and 1903.

In relation to captioning individual pictures, would the book-user (for he is not a reader in the normal sense) need to know much about Greeveguilia or Templegloonthane? Even if we knew the names of the photographers, amateur or artisan (and in many cases we do not), would that information carry any extra reverberation in London or New York? It would be different if the Laurence O'Connor collection had a major significance in the technical history of photography or if individual pictures had the blazing certainty of identifiable masterworks. The captions consequently have a limited ambit and ambition: they attempt to inform but not to suffocate, to accompany without jostling, to respect the fortuity by which the pictures survive.

The collection was formed in Dublin by a Dublin man and its publication originates in Dublin. The city is the book's core and, like Dublin, it images the nation, top-heavily, distortedly, but correctly.

The two hundred and fifty photographs in this book – six or seven per cent of the entire O'Connor hoard – harboured in my house for a brief spell. They became talismanic. Like candle smoke in a dark church guiding a believer to his favourite madonna, a few of the prints demanded return visits, renewed subscriptions of attention.

If only as exorcism, I conjure up a few pictures that would not return easily to their folders. Molesworth Street at dawn, a vanished-within-my-memory pub half-way to the Freemasons Hall; a personal memory of a lively, smiling, unfamous Brendan Behan imposed on the picture, barrelling along the left-hand pavement from the National Library. Next a very quiet dockland scene, men relaxed, cranes immobile. Out west a phalanx of men and boats on the beach at Innismore, energy moving out towards the mainland. Sporting images: a horizontal diver, his dark profile unmistakably Victorian, a class attitude implicit even in mid-air; university athletics in Trinity College, monitored by super-cilious youths in morning dress, the band an expected adjunct. An insolent pale Protestant house, posed pale slum children dirtied up for charity's sake. Fair day bustle in almost nameless towns, the camera angle too wide to admit self-consciousness, small-time cattle and pig people at the nadir of their powerlessness.

My interest in this book, my empathy with it, was initially fused by the conjunction of the selected photographs arriving for perusal and my grandfather's magical manifest of his unknown visage. My wonderment at these particles of the past was equalled by admiration for Mr O'Connor. All those forgotten packets, those delicate dusty plates; the hoping, searching, pouncing; the years of gleaning, the implacable accumulation. His respect for the unknown jobbing photographers hefting cameras and tripods; his connoisseur's eye for the irreplaceable object; and, in the end, this his book, something of lost Ireland that had been slipping away until seized by his certain hand.

Patrick Gallagher, Monkstown, Co. Dublin
June 1984

List of Photographs

The Countryside

Dublin

To the West

The Countryside

Prelude

Still south I went and west and south again,
Through Wicklow from the morning till the night,
And far from cities, and the sites of men,
Lived with the sunshine and the moon's delight.

I knew the stars, the flowers, and the birds,
The grey and wintry sides of many glens,
And did but half remember human words,
In converse with the mountains. moors, and fens.

J. M. SYNGE

At the turn of the century Dingle in County Kerry was an intimate peninsular Irish-speaking town, the last before America. The boys at this pig-fair in 1906 hardly knew the language they spoke was in danger of extinction – nor that their Atlantic promontory was the depository of a fragile literary culture.

I

There was nothing in the least fragile about Killarney House, built by the Earls of Kenmare in the 1870s. Queen Victoria herself suggested the site, dominating the world-famous Lakes of Killarney. This was the ostentatious face of Anglo-Ireland, utterly removed from the Gaelic world of Dingle. An accidental fire totally destroyed Killarney House in 1913.

Four passengers, seated two on either side, back to back: such was the disposition of the notorious Irish outside jaunting car. Victorian travellers reviled at its lack of comfort, revelled in its jarvey's blether. The drivers at Killarney were especially esteemed for their adroit mendacity.

Tralee, county town of Kerry, was the last outpost of normality for Victorian travellers heading for the Celto-Hibernian outback. Globally known for William Pembroke Mulchinock's classic of saccarine song, 'The Rose of Tralee'. The Protestant Mulchinock wrote the ballad for the girl he loved, Mary O'Connor, a Catholic maid-servant. Before they could marry she died of tuberculosis.

4

Headford was the junction for Kenmare. Just up the line was Rathmore Station where there occurred at Christmas time 1896, 'the fearful débâcle of the bog', as the next issue of the Great Southern and Western Railway guidebook was to call it. Two hundred acres of bog 'rolled in a huge mass southwards, sweeping away farmhouses, suffocating the inhabitants and their cattle'. The guidebook, incidentally, was called 'The Sunny Side of Ireland'.

5

Nobody in his own country would back the monorail train patented by the French engineer Charles Lartigue. The British statesman Arthur Balfour threw his influence behind the outlandish idea, with the result that from 1888 to 1924 Lartigue's comic contraption cut a swathe across nine miles of Kerry from Listowel to Ballybunion. To ensure that the carriages were balanced, passengers and iron weights were interchangeable. The company's books never balanced, however; it first went into receivership in 1897.

Below: Another Gallic note. These confiscated lobster pots were shot (in two senses) off Valencia Island around 1905 by French boats illegally fishing Kerry waters. The first Atlantic telegraph cable was laid between Valentia and Newfoundland and the first two trans-Atlantic messages were exchanged on the 5th August 1858, between Queen Victoria and President James Buchanan of the United States. After 271 messages had been sent, faulty insulation made further communications unintelligible. A totally satisfactory cable link was not laid until 1866.

Clusters of circular stone dwellings, known as clachans, at Glenfahan on the Dingle Peninsula. A romantic view of archaeology saw the concentration as 'the Ancient City of Fahan', but the huts probably originated in the eighteenth and nineteenth centuries, indigenous habitations thrown up by a dynamic of settlement.

8

There was no plausible line of historical continuity between the clachans at Fahan and the beehive cells of Early Christian monks. But shelter was an absolute need, stone the ultimate shelter. Shelter for the old anchorite, for the new peasant, for animals and poultry, protection from a scourging ocean.

Wayside dancing in the 1890s at Slea Head, the Ultima Thule of the Dingle Peninsula. The fiddler on the extreme right probably knew a wide variety of traditional airs. This kind of outdoor evening dance continued to the 1940s. It was killed by the motor-car, the commercial dance-hall, and the puritanism of local priests.

10

In the year 1900 the motor ascent to the top of the Windy Gap had a quality of intrepidity. All through the nineteenth century the hills around Killarney had beckoned to the sophisticated traveller. Forelocks were touched, caps readily doffed. The town of Killarney itself all but died of deference to its visitors.

The village of Glengarriff on Bantry Bay was famous for a mild climate and tropical vegetation. The passing bicyclists have perhaps persuaded a quartet of locals to pose. As nimble fingers adjust the apparatus, a second photographer seizes upon the hiatus.

On the 25th October 1866, the death took place in the lovely leafy hill-city of Cork of an important civic office-holder, the Inspector of Hackney Coaches, at the early age of thirty-nine. His grandson, also named James Augustine Joyce, was to chronicle for the world a single day in the life of another Irish city in his novel 'Ulysses'.

Closed shutters and broken windows in Mitchelstown, County Cork, scene of the 'Mitchelstown Massacre' on the 9th of September, 1887. A crowd of 3,000 armed with bludgeons and stones, in the presence of a number of Members of Parliament, attacked the police, who retreated to their barracks. They fired on the crowd from the barracks, killing Michael Lonergan and John Shinnery, and wounding many. The town was quieted by military and the incident did much to move English political sentiment towards the policies of Charles Stewart Parnell.

14

In Victorian Cork the grandest physicians had their room on precipitous Patrick's Hill. Their patients clambered up to them from the city centre below, their complaints aggravated by the one in six gradient. Occasionally messenger boys from the exclusive grocers and wine merchants raced on their delivery cycles to the bottom, all but defying gravity.

Kilkenny in the nineteenth century had a cultural brilliance which was not backed by economic prosperity. As a result, the city and county retained more of their architectural heritage than might have been the case in a richer community. This celebratory occasion involved a Norman tower; the Norman presence in Kilkenny was strong and productive, it's presence felt in village and farm, castle and abbey.

The most recognisable landmark in Waterford City in the last century was Reginald's Tower, close by the busy quays of this eastern port. Reginald MacIvor was an eleventh-century Danish governor of Waterford, but the tower is probably two centuries later.
Below: O'Connell Street in Limerick City, around the turn of the century. The town has never rested easily within the Irish psyche. On the one hand, a reputation for narrow-mindedness and religious bigotry; on the other, strange quirks of merriment. A citizen named William Roche built fabulous hanging gardens behind the street in the 1800s; while out in the countryside at Croom a school of Gaelic poets invented the infectious verse form called the Limerick, which was to be carried across the Irish sea by emigrant workers.

17

18

Punchestown Races in the early years of the century. A few miles from Naas, in the heart of the Kildare horse country, Punchestown was a twice-yearly festival that combined the easy enjoyment of a point-to-point with the hard-nosed professionalism of an Irish Cheltenham.

The motor-car was still a novelty when this was taken near abandoned copper workings at
Bunmahon on the Waterford coast. The car, too, has an abandoned feeling, its passenger
oddly stilted. As sometimes happens in old images, the invisible photographer is strongly
present.

In the days of King John, the town of Tipperary was a centre of Anglo-Norman power. By the nineteenth century it had declined, into a comely agricultural community set in the blue and hazy meadows of Ireland's last Palatinate.

21

Carlow had more zip than Tipperary, as provincial towns went. The Carlovian gentry even had a social club in their main street called the Assembly Rooms. This building was eventually inherited by, of all people, George Bernard Shaw. A special act of parliament had to be passed by Dáil Eireann in 1945 to enable Carlow's most distinguished absentee landlord to bequeath his Assembly Rooms and other unwanted Carlow properties to a bemused but grateful County Council.

The Tighes of Woodstock in County Kilkenny had the best of period taste, an amount of money, and a skilled head gardener in Charles MacDonald. He designed for them a parterre des pièces coupées, 'embroidered in box with a red gravel background'. Years earlier Sarah Ponsonby of Woodstock had scandalously eloped to Wales with her friend Lady Eleanor Butler. They became known as 'the most celebrated Virgins in Europe'.

Simpler folk had simpler pleasures. It's unlikely that a Dubliner today would think of the Vale of Saggart as a suitable venue for an outing, but in the 1890s it was much in vogue. The long exposures necessary then gave a candy-floss artificiality to the babbling brook.

24

Mountmellick was one of the Quaker settlements in what was Queen's County and is now County Laois. The Bewley family employed four hundred in the cotton mills they opened in 1790 and the Pim family enterprises included the old-fashioned bleaching preparation called blue, as well as glue, snuff, candles, tobacco, starch, malting, brewing, baking and tanning. The Bewleys and the Pims were later household names in the commercial life of Dublin.

Mountmellick stood for Quaker diligence; Birr in the neighbouring King's County, now Offaly, for Ascendancy elegance. The Duke of Cumberland stood on his Doric column, vaunting his victory over the Jacobites at Culloden. It was the only unseemly note in a town where pleasing terraces sheltered beneath a fully-functioning family castle.

26

Industrial archaeology from the last century – an unusual horse-drawn coal-crusher, thought to have been somewhere in the Kilkenny area. Possibly associated with one of the very small coal-fields in the Castlecomer district and conceivably used to crush small quantities of coal for a local retail trade.

27

The Dublin and Lucan Electric Railway pre-dated the trams that were to become a feature of the city's streets. This picture shows the route's city terminus on Conyngham Road near the main gates to the Phoenix Park. The journey along the Liffey to Lucan village was a favourite outing.

In 1894 there were over 3,000 fishing vessels on the east coast. One hundred and sixty of these sailed out of Arklow, many of them 45 ton Arklow mackerel boats. Tyrell's boat-building yard gave Arklow an international reputation.

29

Along the northern part of the Leinster coast, clay cliffs alternate with shingle beaches. Wicklow harbour seems to be in permanent decline. Yet the town always provided ratings for the British Navy and Merchant Fleet. Grimsby, Dunverness, Wicklow, Arklow: harsh uncompromising names, concerned with the reality of the sea.

Gorey was a somnolent Wexford town, a farmers town, lying behind sandy beaches and dunes. One of these beaches was at Ardamine. The body of a Chinese sailor was washed up there. Wishing to do the right thing by the unfortunate fellow, advice was taken and he was buried in the Catholic graveyard, carefully pointed towards Mecca.

31

Intrepid navigators, engineers, pioneers. How proud they were, those motorists at the turn of the century. They ran down from Dublin to Woodenbridge in Wicklow, puffing and clattering through the Garden of Ireland, as the county was called, strawberries and beer and good fellowship abounding.

The river Slaney flowing through the substantial town of Enniscorthy in County Wexford. Outside the town was Vinegar Hill, the chief stronghold of the 1798 rebels. When the hill was taken on June 21, the Rebellion was effectively over, but all through the nineteenth century the memory of Wexford and the '98 was at the core of Irish nationalism.

Below: Victorian mills and warehouses proclaimed Enniscorthy's agricultural base. The turreted keep of Raymond le Gros dominated the town. The new cathedral of St. Aidan built by the English architect Augustus Pugin was one of a series of Irish churches which contributed substantially to the contemporary reputation of the leader of the Gothic Revival.

33

34

Blessington in County Wicklow was very much a landlord town, given a royal charter by Charles II in 1669. The rails of a vanished steam tramway curve past a monument to the Downshire family. Small though it was, the town returned two members to the Irish Parliament. When the union of Ireland and Great Britain came into effect on January 1st, 1800, the Marquess of Downshire was paid £15,000 for losing his privilege of nominating the borough's brace of tame parliamentarians.

One of Ireland's most photographed views – the monastic city of Glendalough in the Wicklow mountains. When this photograph was taken, the conical cap on the round tower was new to the landscape. Fallen in for many years it was rebuilt in 1876 using the original stones. A thousand years earlier, an Irish poet had described this monastery dedicated to Kevin, a saintly hermit, as 'a thronged sanctuary'.

36

The Wicklow mountains were a favourite haunt of eighteenth-century travellers in search of the sublime and the picturesque. The Glen of the Downs continued to be admired in Victorian times, the back-drop of the Big Sugar Loaf seeming to block escape from the exuberant vegetation. The Huguenot family of La Touche had embellished the glen with a variety of fashionable follies; a popular diversion was to abandon one's hired vehicle and scramble up the glenside towards an octagonal banqueting-room built on a rocky pinnacle.

The high pass between Glenmalure and the Glen of Imaal had a Himalayan fascination for cycling enthusiasts in the 1880's and 1890's. A popular guide-book wrote: 'The track is terribly severe, and one's machine has actually to be carried for miles!' No wonder the young man pauses before attacking this Wicklow fastness.

38

The early motorist had one advantage over the cyclist on these Wicklow runs. If his route became impassable he at least was not expected to carry his machine. The valley of Glenmacnass was part of a military road built after the 1798 insurrection. It serviced a chain of hill-barracks intended to protect Dublin city.

Glendalough was less wooded in the last century than it is now. Kevin, they say, lived here in a tree and later on a rocky ledge, repulsing women who sought his ascetic company. The reputation of the saint led to the growth of the mediaeval monastery; although remote, it was the point at which a number of mountain routes crossed.

A sheep fair in Rathdrum on the southern route to Glendalough, around 1900. The economy of these Wicklow farmers depended heavily on sheep. Code-marked by their owners, the flocks ranged freely over the mountains.

To certain Victorian observers, taking the pig to market was uproarious Irish comedy. The pig was frequently, however, 'the gentleman who paid the rent' – and that, to the shawled woman in this turn-of-the-century photograph, meant a great deal more than did, say, the coat-of-arms of some landlord family blazoned on the gable wall behind her.

42

These people, too, move on Fair Day with the certainty and vitality of an understood community. Gates, ladders, fencing for sale, a richer farmer on horseback; a Celtic cross asserting a shared belief in the centre of the wide street. It is, of course, nineteenth-century Ireland – but in atmosphere it recalls Central Europe.

An old woman gathering kindling wood in 1890. One of the fuels used in many parts of the country at that time was furze. It continued to be an important source of heat in the areas where turf is scarce, until quite recently. The very poor were driven to use rotten wood from the hedges, straw, stubble and dried horse and cow dungs.

44

A blackthorn-seller wearing the knee-breeches and cutaway coat which all but died out in the later nineteenth century. This photograph was later transformed into a popular postcard showing the blackthorn-seller as a jovial 'Oirishman'.

Outside a Waterford city church, the Virgin watches over these junior dowagers: the children had no eyes for the bent figure stumbling along by the ornate railings.

From inside a country cottage, a welcome for the mother returning from the well or from collecting milk. The forces that kept apart the children in these two pictures began to disintegrate as the new century began.

46

47

The forge on the edge of Enniskerry village was built of good cut stone because the Wingfield family wanted a model village to set off their fine mansion and estate at Powerscourt. The smith repaired implements as well as shoeing horses.

48

Thomas Moore's tree stood proud at Avoca, near 'The Meeting of the Waters', of which the poet – Ireland's national bard – wrote: 'There is not in this wide world a valley so sweet as that vale in whose bosom the bright waters meet.' Time was to reduce the tree to a pathetic stump.

49

Almost all of County Wicklow was beautiful, and Enniskerry was certainly its prettiest village. Associated with the Powerscourt Demesne, the village was all but appropriated by Dubliners who found its healthy Victorian charm a happy antidote to their crowded and unhygienic city.

Many of the boys sentenced to spend time in Glencree Reformatory came from the crowded streets of Dublin. Their place of confinement outside Enniskerry had been a military barracks before this photograph was taken around 1899. One of the presiding Christian Brothers can be seen beyond the circle of young offenders.

This cottage at Lucan in County Dublin was unusual among modest buildings in Ireland. With its hollyhocks, Gothic windows and brick chimneys it represented an imported English vernacular, explained by its propinquity to Guinness estates ranged along the banks of the Liffey.

52

The coming of the railways from Dublin to Bray in 1854 made the watering-place accessible to the city's middle-class. Could the woman in black be James Joyce's governess? In the late 1880s he lived in Martello Terrace, around the corner to the left. His governess, Mrs. 'Dante' Conway, features in his accounts of life in that house. She came from Cork, as did his father, and 'the auntie' spoken in a Cork accent explains her soubriquet.

53

'Repairers are few and far between but the local blacksmiths are often clever and handy men' –
Mecredy's Road Book of Ireland, Dublin, circa 1900.

Fortunately, the jarvey at Enniskerry was usually available. Reluctantly, he would agree to take 'tyre vulcaniser' or 'motor spirit' to a stranded motorist, but he preferred to take his fares around Powerscourt Demesne or, if the weather were suitable, to drive them the ten miles into Dublin itself, to enjoy the delights of the capital.

Dublin

Grey brick upon brick
Declamatory bronze
On the sombre pedestals
O'Connell, Grattan, Moore
And the brewery tugs and the swans
On the balustraded stream
And the bare bones of a fanlight
Over a hungry door.

LOUIS MAC NEICE

In the city, the statue of the Liberator, Daniel O'Connell, was completed in 1882. It backed onto the boulevard which long afterwards was given his name. It also turned its back to Nelson's Pillar, erected in 1808, a monument of which a contemporary wrote: 'Our independence has been wrested from us by the gold of England. The statue of Nelson records the glory of a mistress and the transformation of our senate into a discount office'.

The electric trams gathered like hornets around Nelson's Pillar. They clanged and rattled out to the suburbs, sun-dappled open-decked chargers in summer, steamed-up baccy-smelling slow-coaches in winter.

College Green was one of Dublin's pre-eminent spaces. The wall of the Bank of Ireland, built to house a short-lived parliament, curved towards the flat façade of Trinity College, founded to undermine a long-established religion. High and mighty on his horse, King William III, symbol of religious disunity, seems to disdain both profit and provost.

58

Victorian traffic outside an Elizabethan institution, with Irish citizens of a still United Kingdom circumperambulating the College of the Holy and Undivided Trinity. The university was founded by Queen Elizabeth the First to cut down the numbers of Irish who travelled for their education to France, Spain and Italy, 'whereby they have been infected by popery'.

A jarvey waits patiently for custom under Foley's statue of Henry Grattan. Grattan's had been an eloquent and patriotic voice in the assembly which sat in Parliament House behind him, completed in 1794. Only six years later, the parliament voted itself out of existence, and in 1802 the Bank of Ireland bought the building for £40,000 – less than half its construction cost.

59

60

Early morning in Molesworth Street, looking towards the premises of the Royal Dublin Society, housed in the great mansion of the Dukes of Leinster. The society was founded to help agriculture; it expanded to manage world-famous horse shows; it became a nexus of social activity, a discriminating patron of science and the useful arts.

61

A single-decker tram at the bottom of Grafton Street, the city's most fashionable artery.
The street surface was made of setts, wooden blocks steeped in pitch. The Provost of Trinity
College lived behind the railings; the college itself is further along.

O'Connell Street had been Sackville Street, but after the Liberator's statue went up in 1882
Dubliners unofficially gave his name to the street. In 1891, a French visitor, Madame de Bovet,
had this to say: "It is useless to speak of it to your driver by any other name than that of
O'Connell Street; he will pretend not to understand you". But the shop-keepers were 'west-
British' in outlook and took out a perpetual injunction to restrain the city from officially
changing the name. They had their way until 1926.

Among the many public buildings erected in the eighties was the National Library of Ireland
which evolved from the library of the Dublin Society. James Joyce frequented the reading-
room and the steps between the pillars served as an agora for writers and students. The young
man in the foreground, alone and searching, images Stephen Dedalus in 'Portrait of the Artist as
a Young Man'.

63

64

The street furniture of Dublin was attractive and distinguished. A few paces away from the watery bowers of St Stephen's Green, citizens passing through Kildare Street could feast their eyes on flower-stands of noticeable elegance.

The awkward-looking St Andrew's Church was completed in 1873. Facing it in earlier centuries was the Thingmote, a mound forty feet tall which was the ceremonial meeting-place of the Vikings, from which those early Dubliners promulgated their laws.

66

St Audöen's Arch was the last remaining gateway in the walls of the mediaeval city. In 1879 the gate was restored and the tenement houses huddling against the city wall were demolished.

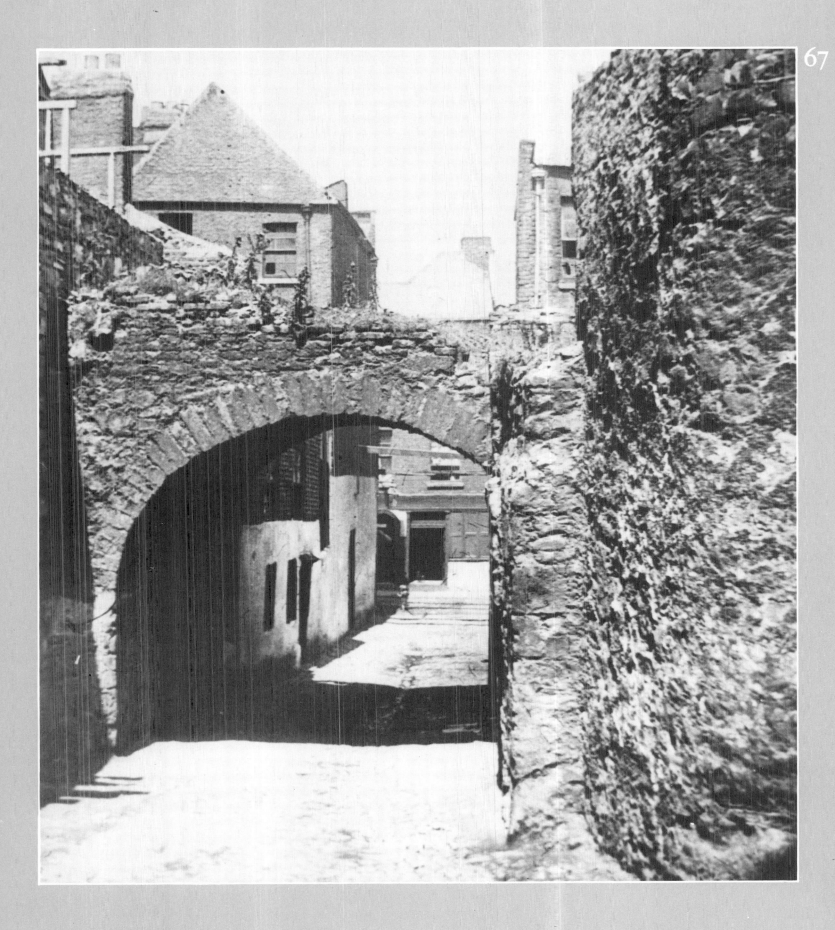

In a city renowned for elegant doorways, this was the tallest and among the most neglected. Once grand enough to house any prime minister, this Number Ten was in Mill Street and graced the one-time dower house of the Brabazon family. This photograph shows the door in its rightful place; in the 1890's the house was, after a fashion, restored, the door taken out and carefully cemented into a wall at the back of the house.

68

The attractive brick-built Weavers' Hall was in the area known as the Coombe, to many the authentic heart of the city. The friendly little monarch in the niche was George the Second. He was made of lead and gilded all over; the gilt wore off, and George became more maniken than monarch.

The city was not short of equestrian statues. This one, on the main road through Phoenix Park, dated from 1880 and commemorated Field-Marshal Hugh Vincent Viscount Gough K.P., G.C.B., G.S.C.I., "an illustrious Irishman, whose achievements in the Peninsular War, in China, and in India, have added lustre to the military glory of this country".

The equestrian image of George the Second had dominated St Stephen's Green for considerably longer than General Gough had been riding into town from the Park. This king had been unveiled in 1758. Although it doesn't look like it in the photograph, the sculptor John Van Nost the Younger depicted the monarch draped in a Roman military habit.

Come, tell me who King Billy was?
Come, tell me, if you can, Sir.
King Billy was a mighty man
In Erin's isle of yore, Sir.

He was, of course, William III, of pious and immortal memory. His statue was unveiled in 1701, on the anniversary of the Battle of the Boyne. When it was finally blown up, the Surgeon-General of the day hastened to the scene, having received a message that 'an important personage had fallen from his horse in front of the Bank of Ireland'.

72

Two centuries later than King Billy, in 1908, Queen Victoria joined the stony images of Dublin town. She sat outside Leinster House, all 168 tons of her, flanked by library and museum, undoubtedly the ugliest statue in the city. Her monumental majesty had been cast by the sculptor Foley in, of all places, gay Paree.

In April 1893, James and Stanislaus Joyce were enrolled as pupils in Belvedere College, the Jesuit day-school which drew many of its pupils from the still fashionable streets that surrounded the north city school.

74

During the eighties and nineties the Royal Dublin Society was developing its showgrounds in Ballsbridge. In 1907 the Society staged a Great International Exhibition on an enormous scale. The exhibition enhanced the attraction of Ballsbridge as a fashionable south city suburb. As the century wore on, more and more of James Joyce's classmates at Belvedere would have had south-side addresses.

Many of the cattlemen who came to the Prussia Street market stayed in the City Arms Hotel, the tall building behind the pens. Elizabeth O'Dowd was the proprietor of the hotel, which Joyceans will recognise as the residence of Leopold Bloom around 1893 or 1894.

Children in the 1890's playing around an old mill on the Poddle River between Blackpits and Sweeny's Lane. Apart from Anna Livia herself, the rivers of Dublin – some of them largely underground – were the Tolka, the Dodder, the Camac, the Bradoge, the Swan, the Poddle and Colman's Brook. There is some flavour of a southern, non-Irish, warmth in this century-old image.

77

Bridge Street existed since 1317. Shortly before the 1798 uprising, practically the entire Leinster Directory of the United Irishmen were arrested in this house. Some of the leaders were liberal Protestants looking for parliamentary reform. Others, like Theobold Wolfe Tone, were influenced by the French Revolution and wished to establish a republic. Their beliefs were potent and long-lasting.

78

Along the quays near the Four Courts, numerous solicitors had their legal offices. Legal stationers followed suit, as here on Wood Quay, later to become known as the site of important Viking archaeological finds. The near-vertical object on the right is a mobile fireman's ladder.

Ireland, having escaped the Industrial Revolution, had no legacy of dark Satanic mills. Dublin, however, had a considerable craft tradition. In the year 1895, the candle manu-facturing firm of Rathbone had already been in existence for no less than four hundred and seven years.

Dublin pubs were formidable in number and diversity. Denis Hayes in Lower Abbey Street was proud of his creamy pint (of Guinness, that is) but that isn't why the pub was soon to take on the name 'The Flowing Tide'. That new name was an echo of Gladstone's reference to 'the flowing tide of Liberal opinion which would make Home Rule a certainty'.

81

The stuccodores who in 1870 festooned a public house on Wood Quay with nationalist decorations were named Burnet and Comerford. Round towers . . . a scene in the Irish parliament . . . a symbolic figure of Erin weeping on her stringless harp . . . Daniel O'Connell. It was not surprising that the bar encased in this patriotic gallimaufry was named the Irish House.

The lady tripping past Lane's pub in Watling Street was heading straight towards Guinness's Brewery. Lane would have sold an excellent pint of Guinness, but his chimney proclaims that he also bottled his own whiskey. The animal on the extreme right is visual corroboration of the adage: 'You can take a horse to the pub, but you can't make him drink'.

83

The sign-writing tradition in the city found a more assured technique here than it did on Patrick Lane's establishment. Yet there is a sense of overkill in both statement and execution. Mr Lane's chimney retained the common touch.

"In 1816 a light and very elegant single elliptic arch of metal was thrown across the river, connecting Liffey Street with the southern side of the city. Foot passengers only can pass it, who pay a toll of one halfpenny". Dubliners called it the Halfpenny Bridge, although it was officially Wellington Bridge. Around the turn of the century, rampant advertising made visual nonsense of that elegant elliptic arch.

85

Indiscriminate control led to . . .

. . . bizarre conjunctions.

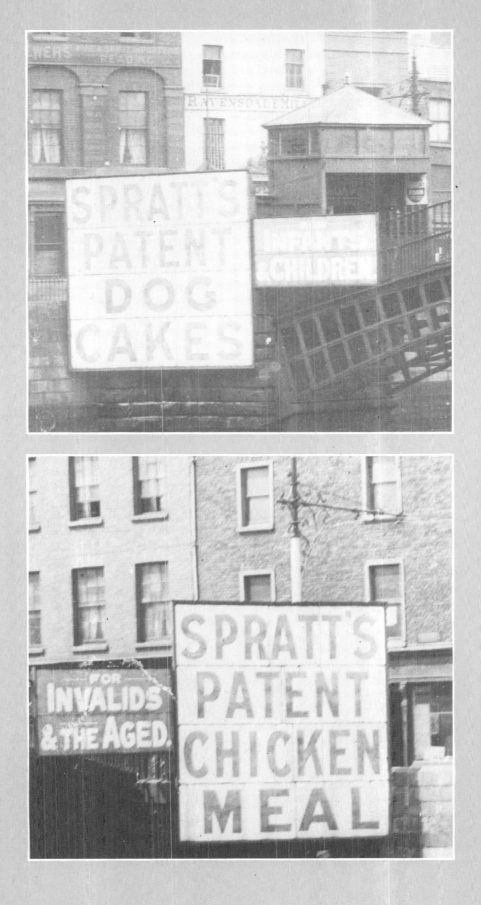

In the last century, huge quantities of turf were carried to Dublin from the sprawling midland bogs. The turf barges exercised a fascination:

'And look! a barge comes bringing from Athy
And other far-flung towns mythologies'.

That was how Patrick Kavanagh later saw such boats as this – a Dublin vessel, number 45B, its owner bearing a well-known Dublin name – Behan.

88

The three locks at the mouth of the Dodder in Ringsend were Camden, Buckingham and Westmoreland. This was Camden, with an elegant Georgian lock-keeper's house. Sailing ships moored a few yards away. Like the Coombe, Ringsend was an area whose inhabitants had a substantial local pride, based on longstanding social cohesion.

Sancton Wood designed Kingsbridge Station for the Great Southern and Western Railway in the mid-1840's. The architectural historian, Maurice Craig, called it 'a delightful building, a renaissance palazzo, gay and full-blooded'. It was also greatly admired by John Betjeman.

Kaiser Bill called the British Expeditionary Force 'this contemptible little army'. As a result, regular army servicemen became known as 'the Old Contemptibles'. After the 1914-18 war some of those veterans founded and staffed the Irish Omnibus Company Ltd. The far-from-contemptible soubriquet was transferred by Dubliners to both the buses and the drivers of the new company, so linking the domestic life of the city to the battlefields where so many of its menfolk had died.

Dublin Corporation refused to erect a statue of Prince Albert, so the widowed Queen Victoria decided not to visit Dublin again. She relented near the end of her life and arrived in 1900, festooned with shamrock. The citizens showed their appreciation by erecting a mock city gate on the Grand Canal Bridge at Leeson Street.

Armed soldiers man a checkpoint outside the City Hall. Scenes like this were not uncommon in Dublin in the early decades of this century. The turning to the right beyond the barricade was an entrance to Dublin Castle, for centuries the seat of British power in Ireland.

93

The large lady in front was no less a personage than Lady Aberdeen, wife of the longest-serving Lord Lieutenant of Ireland. She is attending the opening of the circular Ormonde Market off the quays. The name of one stall – Fingal's Cave – is a reminder of the fashionable Celtic romanticism of the day.

The good Lady Aberdeen was a champion of the poor and dispossessed children of Dublin. This time she attends the opening of a playground in Saint Augustine Street. She also edited a three-volume survey of that ravaging disease of the period – tuberculosis.

Captured cannon from the Crimean War stood outside the Royal Barracks – the oldest barracks in the world in continuous use, dating from 1704. Under the cannon on this patch of ground called Croppies Acre executed rebels of 1798 were buried, many of them headless. Corpses, cannon, pomp, putrefaction.

More cannonballs – at the Royal Hospital at Kilmainham – a sister institution to the one at Chelsea in London. The military pensioners wore a distinctive uniform, and enjoyed a wealth of tradition going back to 1685. It was not for some years after the establishment of the Irish Free State that the surviving pensioners were, in 1927, transferred from Kilmainham to Chelsea. There is every probability that these old men had died long before then.

Hardly a mile from busy Kingsbridge, Sarah Bridge was unexpectedly sylvan in character. The bridge linked Kilmainham to the Phoenix Park at Islandbridge, and was named for Sarah, Countess of Westmoreland, whose husband had been Lord Lieutenant in the 1790's.

98

In the background, Kingsbridge Station stood in all its italianate splendour. In the foreground, the metal bridge over the Liffey built to commemorate the visit of King George the Fourth to Dublin in 1821.

With the dome of Gandon's Four Courts in the background, Queen's Bridge was one of the Liffey's more attractive crossing-points. Named for Charlotte, wife of George the Third, niches and balustrading gave the three-arched structure a quiet dignity.

Guinness barges pass under Victoria Bridge, rebuilt in iron and opened by the Queen in 1863. It had been called Bloody Bridge and was the scene of faction fights between the Weavers or Liberty Boys from the south side of the river and the Butchers from Oxmanstown on the north side.

101

Daniel O'Connell around 1910, by now dwarfed by the eccentric Dublin Bread Company building which towered over the street until destroyed by fire during the 1916 Easter Rising. The open-top electric trams are crowded; their overhead wires contribute to an increasing fussiness in the street.

Until Gandon's Custom House was built, the south quays facing his great building were the usual place of arrival for cross-channel visitors. As time went on, dockland moved east towards the mouth of the Liffey, although smaller trading vessels still used the section of the quay nearest to the city centre.

103

By the early 1900's Belfast had outstripped Dublin as Ireland's leading port. On the south quays of Dublin there was time for older dockers to smoke, watch, remember.

Barrels, sacks of meal, timber . . . the paraphernalia of any port. The biggest import was English coal, even though steam colliers did not appear until 1880. Until then, sailing ships brought the coal to Dublin.

Across the river, the house ensign of a cross-channel shipping company. On the near side, a pitch-and-toss school – an elementary gambling game much favoured by the indolent and indigent. Two coins were flipped from a small wooden board. One enthusiast lies on the ground, the better to monitor his shifting fortunes.

105

106

The workers on the docks lived north and south of the Liffey. The nearest bridge was a long walk up-river. Sturdy ferrymen crossed and re-crossed, busy as water-beetles, charging a tiny amount to keep the supply of labour on the move.

'Uncle Arthur' was the familiar Dublin name for the largest employers – the paternalistic brewing firm of Arthur Guinness, Son & Co. The brewery built Victoria Wharf to accommodate the barges which carried its export porter down to the firm's own ships, en route to the English market.

Generations of Dubliners worked for Guinness's. They rolled and shifted and stacked the barrels, and so did the coopers, the dockers, the draymen, the publicans. A whole European capital seemed to spend an inordinate amount of its time and energy in this thirst-making occupation.

108

109

The south wall of the quays stretched for four miles east into the bay. The cranes swivelled slowly, their giant buckets dipped into unseen holds. And as the century turned, the coins stamped with the face of Victoria rose and fell in that little group of gamblers tensed on the edge of the water.

In many parts of the Victorian city, the countryside edged up to the suburbs. Classon's Bridge over the River Dodder at Milltown had seen the eighteenth century out, and the nineteenth. Judges and merchants and communities of Jesuits lived nearby. Children fished for pinkeens, carrying their catch home in jam-jars, the very jams advertised on the open-top trams whose route ended nearby.

Bullock Castle, in the marine suburb of Dalkey – 'the port of the seven castles'. Gaskin, a local antiquarian, in the third edition (1878) of his 'Irish Varieties' has this quotation: "And castles infinite have been erected long before the advent of the English, standing up like grey wardens, and reproaching the devastating hand of time, but now all tenantless, save to the crannying wind".

The main street of Blackrock, a village on the road to Dalkey, around 1900. A grocery, non-conformist chapel, fire-station, a new free Carnegie library, and a tram service guaranteeing a vehicle every three minutes. To the left of the tram car, the residence of Lord Cloncurry, a marine villa named Maretimo; faintly on the horizon, Newtown House, the home of W. G. Strickland, Registrar of the National Gallery, even then preparing for publication his celebrated 'Dictionary of Irish Artists'.

113

In the early 1900's Rathgar was a most respectable suburb. Later the genteel expression 'Thank God I live in Rathgar' was given popular currency by the comedian Jimmy O'Dea. As in Blackrock, there was a tramline; the Dublin United Tramway Company seemed to be living up to its reputation with no less than three cars in sight. Each route had its special colour, to aid those who could not read. The 1881 census had shown that twenty-three per cent of Dubliners were illiterate.

The city had a wide variety of tranport. The fenestration of this building suggests a club or college. The driver is in darker clothes clutching the reins. The carriage lamp offered safety at night; the high step and the stud wheels offered discomfort in exchange for agility.

115

The four-in-hand was a successor to the coach-and-four, but while the latter might imply one wealthy owner the four-in-hand was a public utility, rare enough even when this picture was taken of ordinary folk bowling along in some style.

This lady was hardly ordinary. It was an age when social judgements were made on the basis of turn-out of your servants, your horses, and your carriage. It may be presumed the house had a grander equipage; at least that is implied by the sheen of the horse, the deference of the servants, and the dowager-like posture of the mistress.

The early 1900's saw the arrival of the motor-car. The three ladies are dressed for a vice-regal garden party but it is hardly conceivable they drove the car themselves. It may have been a delicate early version of topless models draped over gleaming bonnets, or maybe just bonneted models perched in a topless car.

The Gordon Bennett race was the most famous of the early motor-sport events. Dublin's Phoenix Park – the biggest walled park in Europe – was a regular venue for racing. This intrepid pair seem determined enough – but are they even in motion?

From the 1890's on, bicycling enjoyed enormous popularity. The movement at the start of this race is sharply caught. The pistol smoke is fresh in the air; the competitors' assistants unleash pent-up tension.

The premises of the Royal Dublin Society at Ballsbridge were used by the cycling fraternity. These three cornered with élan and their stripped-down cycles suggest a degree of professionalism.

120

121

On a quiet road outside Dublin smartly-attired referees timed a solo sprinter, rather heavily clothed. One local boy applauded; the officials had eyes only for their chronometers and time-sheets.

The excitement mounted as the gallent solo sprinters ran the gamut of a sporting bureaucracy. Local women with their shopping bags, faced with these rocket-like speedsters, hugged the grass verge.

122

123

Spooning up some magical bicyclists vitamin mixture? The Irish cycling magazines of the 1890's don't provide the answer, but they do advertise bicycles of merit at the price of "gas pipe contraptions". Even bicycles-made-for-two.

In R.J. Mecredy's popular magazine 'The Irish Cyclist' advertisements appeared for " Celebrated Referee Clothing: Norfolk Suits, Rain but not Air-proof; Referee Hose, Referee Caps, Sweaters, Ponchos and Shoes – as worn by ALL the world's greatest riders." Could these few photographs be merely advertisements? Even so, what is this chap eating, and again from an outsize dish? And do they know about the Peeping Tom?

124

125

What was going on here? In his 'Road Book of Ireland', R.J. Mecredy hinted at an answer. "Intercourse with the peasantry will be found interesting and amusing. For those who are not particular it will be found an excellent plan to lunch in their cottages. There is little use questioning them as to distances, however. They are nearly always wrong and in any case they calculate in Irish miles."

Ringsend was where the packet boats came in, before the silting of the Pigeon House harbour forced them to move to Howth or Dun Laoghaire. Until then Ringsend had been prosperous and was in the 1890's not only the packet boat terminus but also the headquarters of the Dublin fishing fleet — and of all the city's rowing clubs.

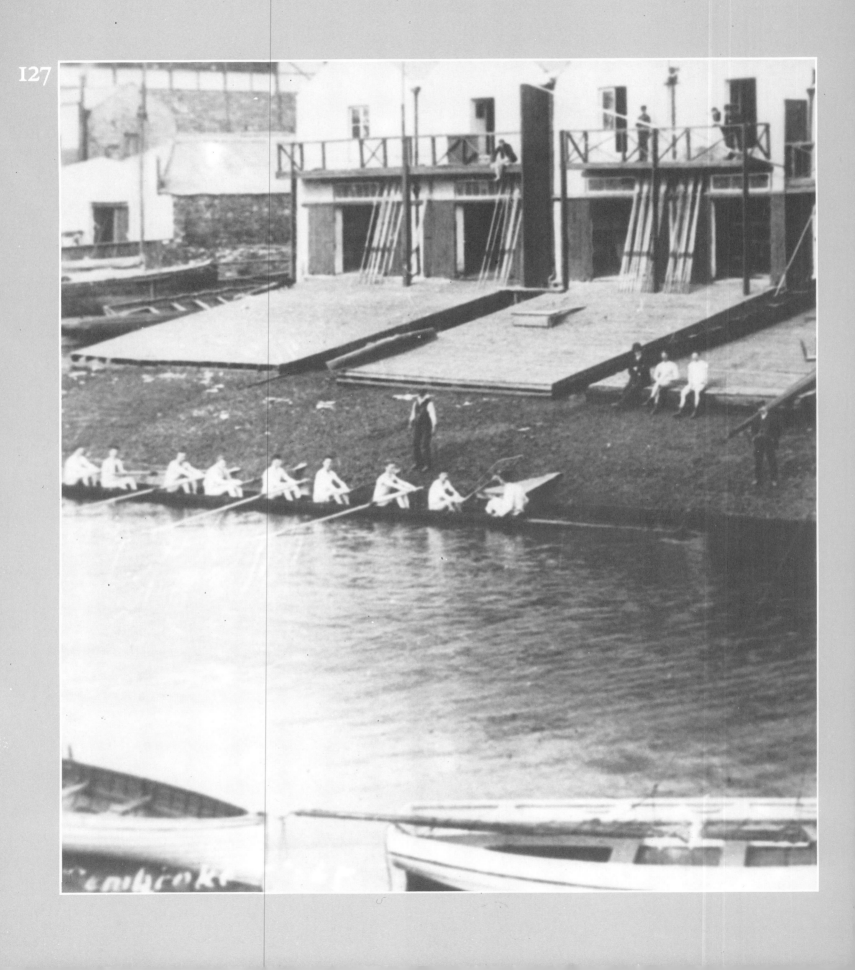

The massive cut stone suggests the South Wall built under the direction of Captain Bligh of the Bounty and stretching out into Dublin Bay. Trick diving or trick photography?

From whence did this Edwardian daredevil spring? In or on what element did he land? His profile has the mustachioed disdain of the officer class. His friends carry resentment. Or are we simply looking at the darkroom jokes of an early photographic club?

College Week in Trinity College Dublin at the turn of the century was a mixture of student dandyism and genuine sporting endeavour. This player appears to have an almost nonchalant confidence. Like some of the very greatest players, he is left-handed.

The College Races were a highlight of College Week. Wits like Oliver Gogarty could run, box, motor, fly – and write crystalline verse in Greek or Latin. A boatered clergyman, an attentive professor, undergraduate stewards.

He sprinted to the mark, jumped. A very smart judge at this end made sure he had not crossed the line. Another judge will measure how long his jump was. Later he may have strawberries and cream with the Provost's wife or beer with the Knights of the Campanile. And the band will play once more, for this is College Week and the young gentlemen are enjoying themselves.

Some better Dublin houses had archery ranges. Lord Iveagh, head of the Guinness family, had one in the gardens of the mansion he was to give to the Irish Free State to house its Department of External Affairs. Father waits as his slim-waisted daughter holds her bow in readiness for the photographer's instruction. Her beau is an attendant lord, his dog is at her side. The grapes ripen in the conservatory; it was summer in Dublin.

These gymnasts were in 1908 members of the Fishamble Street Gym Club. The club was located in the heart of the old city in the street where Handel's 'Messiah' had its first performance in 1742. On the Sabbath Day the Fishamble Street Club became a Sunday School.

134

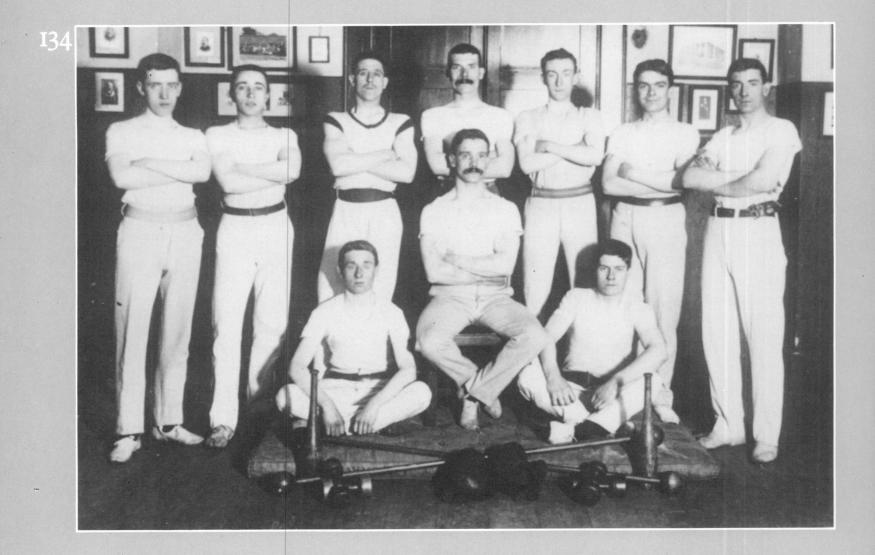

Twenty men of Dublin town gathered to pose for this photograph, possibly the sole surviving testimony to their activity. But what was that activity? At least seven styles of dress: walking-sticks a-plenty – and two shepherds crooks. A fashion show for a military and gentlemens tailor? Or perhaps the staff of the Vice-Regal Lodge?

Three generations – or maybe four. The essence of Dublin was to be found in its older citizens. Increasingly after 1900, migrants from the provinces added to the city's population. They had little sense of its closely-knit loyalties, its humour, its dignities.

Looking pretty relaxed – but is grandmother camera-shy?

A hilly picnic site – Howth, maybe, or the Scalp near Enniskerry in County Wicklow. Sandwiches, and a fine big teapot. Are these the three girls we already met in a swanky motor car?

At some event – possibly a gymkana or sports meeting, the man glancing at a programme.

139

The children of the slums enjoyed no picnics. Photography was used by humanitarian interests to draw attention to the appalling living conditions of working-class people.

The middle-class who attended Sunday School activities in Fishamble Street were within spitting distance of festering poverty. Lady Aberdeen led a campaign against spitting as a cause of tuberculosis.

Frequently the tenement houses were the former houses of upper class, even aristocratic families. Shawled women sat by panelled doors: older women tried to keep up appearances. In 1911, 41.9 per cent of deaths in the Dublin Metropolitan area occurred in workhouses, lunatic asylums, and other institutions.

Some children were happy, even in the tenements; but statistics showed that infant mortality between the ages of one and five was 0.9 per thousand among the professional classes; for artisans it rose to 4.8, reaching 12.7 among the children of hawkers, labourers and porters.

142

143

Forbes Cottages huddled under a warehouse. The nationalist leader Michael Davitt found many such households headed by women, who paid an average rent of two shillings and a penny-farthing from a total income of eight shillings and sixpence per week.

Angle Court was much the same as hundreds of city corners, but it was perhaps less unhygienic for a family to live in a courtyard like this than to occupy one room on the third or fourth floor of a decaying Georgian mansion.

Cross-stick Alley acquired its name in 1758. In 1910 this backwater off Meath Street showed every sign of dereliction and despair. Any slum clearance that was done was carried out by commercial interests such as the railway companies.

In the 1870's attempts were made to reduce the incidence of prostitution in certain areas of the city. Yet when Joyce came to write 'Ulysses', Dublin still had a flourishing night-town. Brady's Cottages had no especial reputation: the corruption and misery were widespread.

146

147

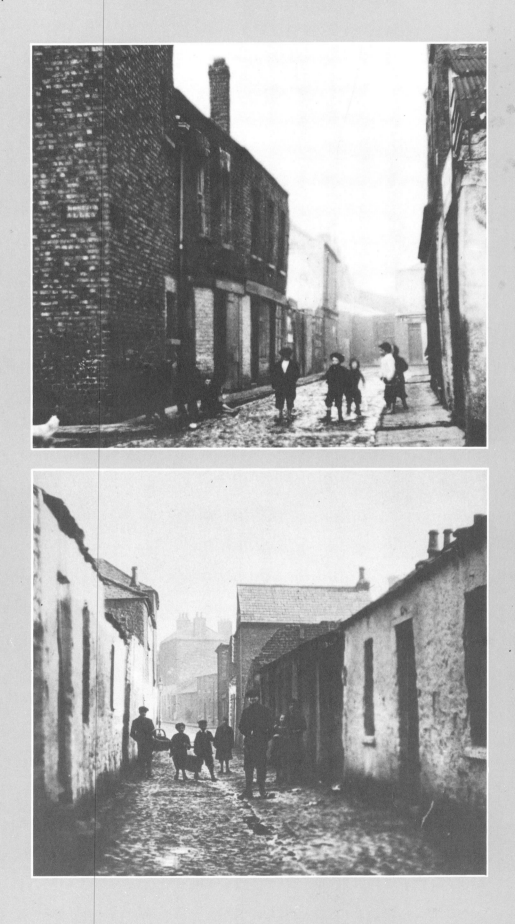

The attitude of the churches towards state relief for poverty was conservative. The problems of casual labour and chronic unemployment were avoided by church and state.

In yards like Morgan's Cottages sanitary facilities were minimal. Dublin Corporation had regulations about closet accommodation but the city analyst, Sir Charles Cameron, argued that to enforce the regulations would mean closing many houses, leaving the tenants homeless.

The new cells provided under the Bridewell at the Four Courts were described in 1905 as being 'commodious and well-suited to the purpose.' They also allowed the prisoners to prompt their lady friends towards necessary action.

150

The famous Theatre Royal was situated in Smock Alley. The beautiful and famous Gunning sisters had lost both money and credit, in which difficulty their mamma called in Mr Thomas Sheridan, the manager of the theatre. He kindly allowed the handsome sisters to choose from the rich wardrobes of his green-room, and in this way they were enabled to go to the 'Drawing Room' across the road in Dublin Castle. By such means they became Lady Coventry and the Duchess of Hamilton.

Engine Alley began its long life as Indian Alley. Living around here in 1900 were labourers, porters, small dealers, pedlars, hawkers, charwomen, rag-pickers, night-watchmen, the inferior class of seamstresses, and sandwich men.

152

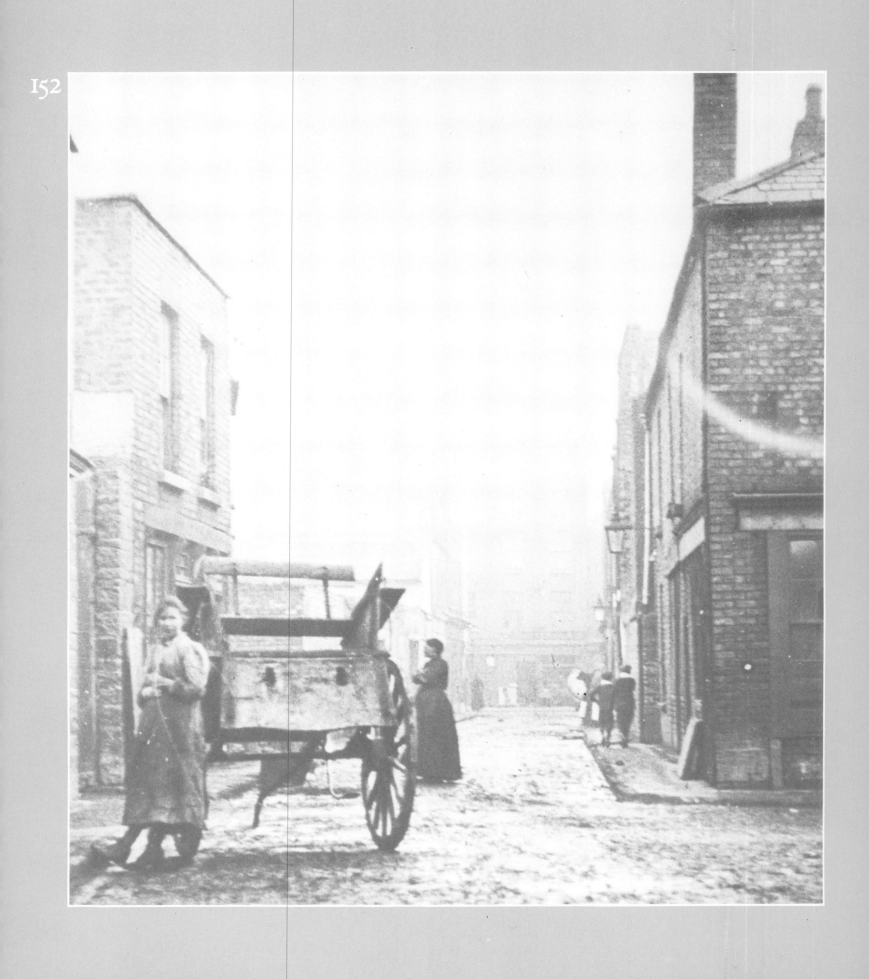

The coffin-makers lived in Cook Street. Not so far away in Faddle Alley lived the anarchic blind ballad-singer Michael Moran, known as Zozimus. He knew all about coffins, and about mortality.

'I live in Faddle Alley
Off Blackpits near the Coombe
With my poor wife, Sally,
In a dirty nasty room.'

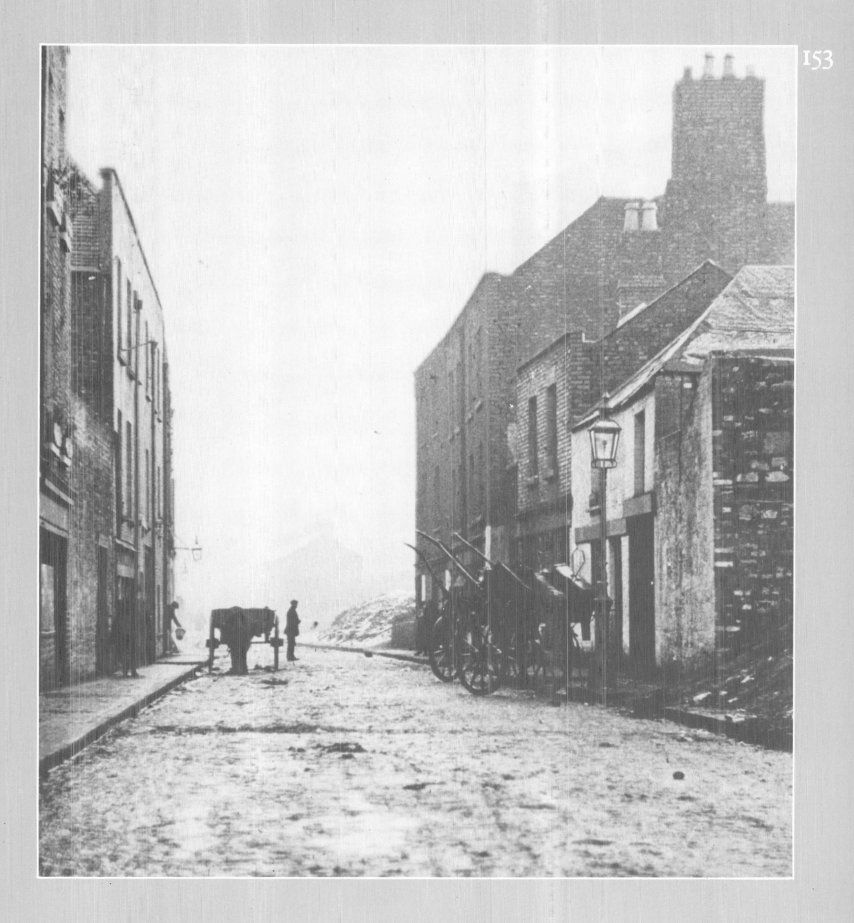

153

The charladies of the city were elemental and celebrated. Alma Luvia Pollabella, the washerwomen at Chapelizzard. O'Casey created Juno, Joyce his Molly Bloom, and Jimmy O'Dea never stopped singing that Biddy Mulligan was the Pride of the Coombe.

154

In all likelihood, these women are waiting for a pawnbroker to open his premises. In on Monday, out for Sunday. A few shillings for the husband's suit or her own best shoes. The money needed to feed the baby, the clothes wanted back for Sunday Mass.

Yet there was time for love. Kind lady loved baby...

. . . brother loved sister.

Outside the city, things were hardly different for the poor. These cottages at Rathfarnham cowered behind a big house that had belonged to the King's Printer and later to the Order of Loreto.

Kings, clerics, and in this lost Ireland there were also the heroes. Among them Robert Emmet, whose family owned this house called Casino in Clonskeagh. Rebel leader, insurrectionist, romantic hero.

The garden at Casino led to a bower which Emmet used as a study. Beneath, there was a tunnel through which to escape when danger threatened.

> 'But I was arrested and cast into prison.
> Tried as a traitor, a rebel, a spy;
> But no one can call me a knave or a coward,
> A hero I lived and a hero I'll die'.

159

160

Wolfe Tone was borne in Stafford Street, the son of a coachmaker. He persuaded the French to mount a naval expedition to Ireland, was captured, and died by his own hand. Tone was life-enhancing and witty, a magnetic revolutionary.

His grave at Bodenstown became a Republican shrine.

'For Tone is coming back again, with legions o'er the wave,
The scions of Lord Clare's Brigade, the dear old land to save.
For Tone is coming back again, with legions o'er the wave,
The dear old land, the loved old land, the brave old land to save.'

161

162

They waited in the drenching rain at two o'clock on Sunday, October 11, 1891 outside their City Hall. "An uncovered man appeared on the balcony, cried out, "Hush, Hush", and instantly there was deep silence and heads were uncovered and what was before a black, indistinguishable mass became a sea of white, anxious, and sorrowful faces." The funeral of Parnell had begun.

163

'It was nearly half-past six when, at last, in the wet dusk, he was buried.'

'Say now to Emmet and Wolfe Tone, moreover –
Who hold their hands to you –
That never your Ireland had a better lover
Then you your Ireland slew.'

164

In 1899, the foundation stone of the Parnell Monument was laid in O'Connell Street. Huge crowds attended the unveiling. It was said of Parnell that he was the corner-stone of the Irish arch, and that when it fell, he fell. He was the lost leader of the lost Ireland this book remembers.

To the West

Stone-walled cabins thatched with reeds,
Where a Stone Age people breeds
The last of Europe's stone age race.

JOHN BETJEMAN

Exploring the Shannon lakes by steamer was a popular way of experiencing the acceptable face of Victorian Ireland. The 'Countess Cadogan' chugged along the Duke of York Route from Killaloe in County Clare to Dromod in County Leitrim.

From Killaloe the steamers ranged north through Lough Derg to Portumna.

'Portumna's towers, Bunratty's regal walls,
Carrick's stern rock, the Geraldine's grey keep.
Rivers of dark mementoes! must I close
My lips with Limerick's wrongs – with Aughrim's woes?'

Long before the strutted railway bridge was built over the Shannon at Athlone, the defence of the town's original bridge had become part of the national myth. Schomberg, the Williamite general, sent a messenger to Colonel Richard Grace to offer him immunity if he surrendered. Grace was playing cards and wrote on the six-of-hearts: 'It ill becomes a gentleman to betray his trust'. That card became 'Grace's Card' to patriotic Irishmen.

Athlone again, on a fair day in the 1890's. The boy wearing a hat in the centre might have been on his way to visit a school-friend who lived in a side-street to the left. The friend, born there in 1884, was John McCormack. Indeed, the boy in the hat might be the world-famous singer.

This was Mullingar, a town a few miles from Athlone, in 1895. A curious oddity linked the two towns. John McCormack's runner-up in a prestigious singing contest was James Joyce, who spent the summers of 1900 and 1901 in Mullingar. Perhaps for that reason, in 'Ulysses' he exiled young Milly Bloom, fourteen-year-old daughter of Leopold and Molly, to the town — maybe because Milly was having incestuous relations with her father while in Dublin.

170

The main street of Longford town, in the late 1800's. Agricultural, inland, undistinguished. Boys in knickerbockers, a donkey, a clear skyline.

Longford, the same street, in the early 1900's, only slightly changed. A boy of the same age, but wearing short pants; a bicycle; telegraph posts. Still agricultural, inland, undistinguished.

172

Seaweed was collected from the foreshore: it could be eaten, burned to produce a fertiliser, or used to manure the soil. On the Dublin coast, the village of Rush was a fish-curing centre.

Working at low tide on the Rush trawlers. One fish from Rush had a reputation as a local delicacy – the ling. The sandy soil along this coast encouraged a group of bulb-growers from Holland.

Until the early years of the century and the general availability of electric power, windmills to grind corn were common enough on the eastern coast. This one at Skerries, near the village of Rush, dominated an area associated with the early months of Saint Patrick's mission to Ireland, in the year 432.

175

In the year that Patrick was in Skerries, he also crossed the Boyne at the ford of Trim and founded a monastery by the Boyne water. The Norman Abbey of S. Mary was founded around 1250 on the same site: this is all that remained of the abbey's fine Yellow Steeple after Cromwell's guns had wreaked their havoc.

Near the abbey was an immense fortress built by the powerful Hugh de Lacy. A motor-car simply drove through a gateway in the curtain-wall. Earlier intruders had to deal with the complexities of portcullis and barbican.

Hello, sailor! A young visitor to Tara in County Meath – Ireland's royal acropolis – is greeted by the Penis of Fergus, a standing stone which Victorians preferred to call the Stone of Destiny.

The walls of Drogheda, capital of Royal Meath, failed to withstand Cromwell in 1648. The few inhabitants he didn't massacre were shipped to Barbados. "I am persuaded that this is a righteous judgement of God upon these barbarous wretches."

Ninety feet above high water on the Boyne, the railway viaduct at Drogheda stalks across the river-mouth. The trains were barely audible inside the low thatched cottages.

178

179

180

In the estuary of the Boyne below Drogheda coracles were used by net-fishermen hunting salmon. As old as any craft in Europe, the oval coracles, originally made from cow-hide, were propelled by a single paddle. Tarred canvas covered a framework of osiers, or hazel wands.

181

The towns of Ulster are subtly or broadly shaded by religion and politics. Omagh is in County Tyrone. This 1890's photograph of its dipping high street has the linear clarity of an engraving.

182

On the other side of the province, and in the golden days of Good Queen Bess, one Rose Whitechurch took one Edward Trevor as her husband. They called their estate Rostrevor, and outside this County Down seaside town is an obelisk to the memory of a local soldier, Major-General Ross, who distinguished himself in 1814 at the Battle of Bladenburg when his outnumbered force defeated the Americans, thus allowing the British to sack Washington and burn the White House.

Until the very late 1800's, only the committed traveller visited great stretches of the Irish coast. This fishing scene in County Donegal repeated itself behind each headland, revealing a way of life all but unknown to city-dwellers.

A bare-footed woman spins in her cottage yard at Fair Head in County Antrim, the nearest point in Ireland to Scotland. Spinning and weaving boosted minimal agricultural earnings: this work was always done by women.

Out west in County Mayo, the town of Westport had the air of landlord patronage. In the Octagon, a memorial to a benefactor, Lord Glendinning. Regency detailing could not soften the horrors of the Great Famine that came in the 1840's.

"A fine little town in a splendid setting; a tree-lined mall, wide streets, a theatre by Wyatt in a charming octagon." And then the troubles came, not only to Westport, but to all of the west.

In the cottages an old way of living continued. The big spinning wheel was used to ply wool for knitting purposes or sometimes, with certain changes, to wind the yarn on to bobbins for use by the weaver.

The weekly market in the towns of Connemara was no more than a commercial necessity – yet the retrospect of a century has given to wickerwork, clothing, and the accoutrements of animals the sharper focus of social history.

A rough tripod supported the weighing scales. The multi-coloured plaid shawls were standard womens garb in the early 1900's but in time became more associated with travelling tinkers than with the countryside community.

189

190

A lakeside cottage in County Galway in 1900. Rivulets on the mountainside . . . the sparkle of quartz in sunshine . . . the sense of isolation by water . . . all the romantic traveller desired.

Social reality had a harder edge. Every ruined cottage in County Mayo meant a family gone, part of a local fabric torn. The greater part of emigration from the west was to the United States. In a landscape like this, Cleveland was merely over the hill.

It was hard to keep the ties with home when all in a townland had gone. England, and America, swallowed up the defeated, the dispossessed. The modes of a culture could to some extent be transferred, but the misty desolation of home could only be left to a final decay.

192

193

Peat or turf was the natural countryside fuel. The abundant lowland bogs were worked by hand, the men cutting, the women and children drying and stacking the sods. The cutaway bog was a wild and airy place; it ventilated the imagination of a highly literate rural society.

Landlords in the 1870's had too many tenants. Wanting to clear their congested estates and give more land to grazing, they intensified a policy of evictions. This group was photographed in County Clare in the context of an eviction, but while the foreground figures may indeed be bailiffs, the status of the background chorus has a cinematic ambiguity.

195

The motor-car opened the west of Ireland to the well-to-do visitor. The drive along Killary
Harbour was much enjoyed – a fjord-like inlet at Leenane in County Galway which on occasion
had provided moorings for squadrons of the Royal Navy.

The sense of inland Connemara was well represented by quiet guest-houses in such places as Maam, known to nineteenth-century English visitors for the lure of its hills, the hint of salmon in its streams, and the general delectation of its scenery.

197

Clifden, a town of no great antiquity, became the chief town of Connemara. Market day had an air of relaxed activity. Donkeys, panniers, knitted caps, decorative shawls, tweed trousers . . . ingredients of what was to become identi-kit Ireland.

Time was to make of Oughterard in Connemara a quietly fashionable retreat, an area of fishing and shooting lodges for well-to-do Dubliners. In the 1880's the journey to and from Sunday Mass was still for local people social ritual, family relaxation, religious duty.

198

199

In later years the architecture of Irish towns became a subject of study. As in any building convention that evolved naturally, the relationships between slate and thatch, whitewash and stucco were subtly modulated.

In the late 1890's citizens of Galway gathered at the quay-side fish market, waiting for the Claddagh boats to bring in the catch. The archway partially visible on the left was one of four such arches built in 1594 to protect cargoes when Spanish ships were unloading.

200

201

A variety of transport, but as yet no mechanically-propelled vehicle. Although public and political life went on, at times tumultuously, quotidian life in the west remained virtually unchanged for many decades.

The Tourists Picturesque Guide to Kilkee in the year 1873 tells us that sermons in Irish were still preached to the rural congregation in this fashionable holiday place. And that "the western portion of the shore is reserved for ladies. The rougher sex seek the refreshing plunge at Burn's Cove." In 1842 Tennyson mooched around here alone, having failed to contact his fellow-poet Aubrey de Vere.

The Victorian concerns of coastal resorts like Kilkee had nothing at all to do with life on the Atlantic islands. The Aran Islands had no native fuel; turf was ferried to them in Connemara hookers, unique sailboats of long lineage which moved along the Western coastline with the archaic ease of caiques among the Cyclades or dhows in Arabian waters.

203

204

The Galway or Connemara hooker was a 'black-bellied and brown-sailed' boat-of-all-work, about 35 feet long, 'a half-decked, single-masted, gaff-rigged vessel with a bowsprit, carrying a large mainsail and jib'. In earlier times, they were said to have sailed from Galway to France and the Channel Islands smuggling brandy and other dutiable delectables.

Away to the North was Tory Island. West Town was one of the two villages on the island, eight Atlantic miles off the north-westerly tip of Ireland. Resilient, inhospitable, remote; before Christian times, the haunt of the pirate Balor, he of the evil eye. In the sixth century Saint Columcille founded a monastery at West Town; a crumbled round tower survived centuries of Atlantic gales.

206

The curraghs used on Tory differed from those in Galway or Kerry. They had a leaner profile and distinctive paddle-shaped oars. Islanders also used a mini-curragh barely eight feet long, manoeuvred by its one-man crew paddling while kneeling in the bow.

The rolling mountains of Achill Island in County Mayo sheltered a population whose economy was sustained by migratory labour to a much greater degree than that of other islands. For part of each year, Achill, the largest of the Irish islands, was a community of women. The men travelled in groups to work on the potato harvest in Scotland and parts of Northern England.

In 1887, Achill was linked to the mainland, thus opening its fifty square miles of wild beauty to a distinctive type of discriminating visitor. Amateur naturalists and geologists responded to the compulsive attraction of the island. From its simple hotels motor expeditions set out in search of the amethyst stone which was to be found in certain known locations.

208

209

In the 1880's the inhabitants of Clare Island off County Mayo steadfastly refused to pay rent to their landlords, an obduracy possibly inherited from the sixteenth-century lady pirate Grace O'Malley, whose castle overlooks the island's harbour. By the turn of the century, the Congested Districts Board had taken over the island and implemented much-needed agricultural reform.

Clare Island had a pastoral ease despite its exposed situation in Clew Bay, hardly twenty miles from the town of Westport. An elaborate scientific survey of the island in the early 1900's found many animals and plants which were not only unrecorded in Ireland or Great Britain, but were unknown to science. This pony disguised as a haycock did not fool the researchers from the Royal Irish Academy.

210

211

Of all the Irish islands, the three Aran Islands were the most known. In the very early twentieth century, John Millington Synge placed them in literature, and later Robert Flaherty gave filmic form to their distinctive way of life. On the middle island, Inishmaan, groups waiting on the beach for the steamer to arrive had the quality of players in readiness, a curtain about to rise.

And on the boat, as it steamed from Galway city into Aran, men and women from the islands crowded the deck, sharing space with a few visitors who were drawn by a Gaelic way of living, by a remote society on the edge of Europe.

212

213

For half-a-century Aran's link to the mainland was the tough little steamer called the Dun Aengus, the name of a huge stone fort on the largest island. The steamer was the best-known of Ireland's coastal vessels: it had a quality of indomitable obstinacy. Its crew were as family to the islanders, bearers of post, packages, gossip.

In the 1930's Robert Flaherty was to make his classic film 'Man of Aran'; Sean Keating was painting island stereotypes; and Liam O'Flaherty writing stories that told the world about his birthplace. Synge had already in prose and drama introduced the islanders to the world stage.

215

Livestock was brought in on the steamer. Winching a horse ashore at Kilronan, the post-village on Inishmore – the biggest island – was comparatively simple. On the smaller islands, when there was no pier for the steamer, she lay offshore and the animals were towed ashore behind curraghs.

Pigs for sale on the mainland being escorted to the harbour: the woman carried sacks and bundles. A man's working life moved between fishing from the shore, attending to his fields by his house, and supervising his rough grazing near the sea-cliffs at the back of the island.

216

217

The curraghs met the steamer when it stopped some distance off-shore at Inishmaan. In many parts of the world this scene was accompanied by excited touting and selling of wares, but not on Aran.

Curraghs carried sacks of export potatoes, grown in tiny fields rescued from the rocks, 'made' land as it was called. The potato famines had little effect on the islands, which fell back on a fish diet during periods of shortage.

This photograph has a classical sense of immediacy. The boats ferried the sacks to the steamer, invisible pivot of the action.

Handling curraghs demanded great skill. One man told Synge: "A man who is not afraid of the sea will soon be drowned . . . But we do be afraid of the sea, and we do only be drowned now and again."

220

221

Respect for the sea was central to island life – and that frequently meant waiting and patience. Even on a calm day, the arrival of the steamer was unpredictable, allowing time for desultory relaxation.

Again, on the beach at Inishmaan waiting. The plaid shawls tied over the head, the younger women bare-headed. Boys with wide-peaked tweed caps, cattle for sale on the mainland. And, noticeably, wicker baskets of various sizes.

A jaunty cavalcade of islanders, fully aware of the camera's presence. Thatched cottages, stone walls, outcrops of rock: a homogenous range of colour, a rootedness.

224

The girl posed unaffectedly, turf panniers beside her. Up to a certain time the islanders found no intrusion in the interest of strangers.

A more casual image. This woman wore a crochet shawl, the man in the wide-brimmed hat supported his substantial tweed trousers with the traditional multi-coloured belt called a crios.

226

Patriarchal, intent on his task, which perhaps was to whitewash a cottage wall. He may be carrying a quantity of lime in the sack over his shoulder.

In the Proceedings of the Royal Irish Academy, xxxiii, 1916–17, pp. 530–8, the remarkable Dr. J. P. Mahaffy contributed a paper 'On the Introduction of the Ass, a Beast of Burden, into Ireland' in which he suggested that donkeys became popular as pack-animals in Ireland during the Napoleonic Wars when horses were in great demand for the British campaigns in Spain.

228

Two baskets or panniers hung from a wooden pack saddle, or straddle. Under the panniers were protective mats usually woven from straw. A belly rope, a crupper rope around the animal's tail, and a simple bridle completed the harness.

The pannier baskets were used as back-packs by animals and humans alike. Some had a hinged bottom to release the load without unharnessing the animal. Creel or kesh, dung pot or pardog, pannier or basket – whatever the terminology, these wickerwork containers were ubiquitous.

Man, boy, pony. Tweed hat, waistcoat jacket, pampooties – sandals made of hide, softened in sea-water, supple on the sharp rock.

Men, boys, little boy. The little boy on the chair is dressed as a girl, the usual island custom to a certain age.

232

Mother and daughter (or son). Island women often wore long scarlet skirts. The crimson material was woven on the islands, was later imported, and in time gave way to staider indigo. Her sash is a local crios.

Every process in the making of traditional clothing was carried out on the islands – from preparing the newly-cut wool to spinning, weaving and tailoring.

233

234

Nimble fingers were needed to make a crios, the islands' distinctive belt or sash. No loom was used, the threads tied to one foot. Six colours between white edgings, plaits at each end, three yards long or more for a man, two for a woman.

The big spinning wheel in this picture was gradually replaced by a much smaller type called the flax wheel. Unmarried women were expected in early times to spin enough yarn for a trousseau, hence the meaning of 'spinster'.

The women of Aran were hard-working, and in the frequent absence of their men in America or England, they acquired a notable matriarchal status.

236

237

Around 1890, these boys stood for a society that seemed immutable. The skirts worn by the younger boy echoed age-old social custom. Yet in 1896 a writer was born in Aran – Liam O'Flaherty – who was to give a cosmopolitan context to these remote islands.

Indoors, the iron cauldron hanging from the swinging crane; the smouldering turf; the kettle in readiness; and an old woman spinning yarn. Old ways, old work – and an old language.

Outdoors, an old woman working. The thatch tied to spiggots in the wall against storm winds; the loose-stone wall; whitewash on rough plaster; a culture stopping, a strong woman's face looking into uncertainty.

Away from the house, out on the rocks, a boy gathering seaweed, to burn to make kelp, sold to produce iodine; or kept to 'make' new land between the stones where nothing grew before. A glowing culture and a scant subsistence; the contrast and glory and sadness of the Aran Islands. In all Ireland, only two outposts stranger, more extreme.

241

The Great Blasket Island, off the Dingle Peninsula, off the coast of Kerry, 'next parish to America'. Small islands that gradually depopulated, a tiny community that produced books of near genius.

242

Ninety years ago, a postman landing on the Blaskets, carying news from the world; and a woman visitor arriving in this isolated place, to find in its language and folklore rhythms as old as any in Europe.

The Great Blasket Island, off the Dingle Peninsula, off the coast of Kerry, 'next parish to America'. Small islands that gradually depopulated, a tiny community that produced books of near genius.

Ninety years ago, a postman landing on the Blaskets, carying news from the world; and a woman visitor arriving in this isolated place, to find in its language and folklore rhythms as old as any in Europe.

243

Fifteen hundred years ago, six hundred feet above the sea, eight miles out in the Atlantic, a community of Christian hermits lived on the Great Skellig island off the Kerry coast. They pared existence to a minimum: they maximised the spiritual and called to God from their eyrie. They pre-dated all of this book, those craggy mystics, yet their strange Ireland lies behind so many of the later images . . . behind the monasteries and the towns, behind the life of the islanders, the authority of the rich, the desperate optimism of the city poor. Those monks call to us and to all of lost Ireland.

244